# Word Origins

**John Butterworth**

Illustrations by Lee Nicholls

OXFORD

UNIVERSITY PRESS

# OXFORD
## UNIVERSITY PRESS

Great Clarendon Street, Oxford OX2 6DP

Oxford University Press is a department of the University of Oxford.
It furthers the University's objective of excellence in research, scholarship,
and education by publishing worldwide in

Oxford  New York

Athens  Auckland  Bangkok  Bogotá  Buenos Aires
Cape Town  Chennai  Dar es Salaam  Delhi  Florence  Hong Kong  Istanbul
Karachi  Kolkata  Kuala Lumpur  Madrid  Melbourne  Mexico City  Mumbai
Nairobi  Paris  São Paulo  Shanghai  Singapore  Taipei  Tokyo  Toronto  Warsaw

with associated companies in  Berlin  Ibadan

Oxford is a registered trade mark of Oxford University Press
in the UK and in certain other countries

Text copyright © John Butterworth 2001
Illustrations copyright © Lee Nicholls 2001

The moral rights of the author have been asserted

First published 2001

British Library Cataloguing in Publication Data available

ISBN 0–19–910750–5

1 3 5 7 9 10 8 6 4 2

Designed and Typeset by Mike Brain Graphic Design Limited
Printed in China

**Acknowledgements**

The editors and publishers gratefully acknowledge permission to reproduce the following
copyright material:

Geoffrey Chaucer: 'The Knight's Tale', lines 1467–9 and 'The Pardoner's Tale', lines 870–2,
from *The Complete Works of Geoffrey Chaucer*, edited by F.N. Robinson,
copyright © F.N. Robinson, 1957. Reprinted by permission of Oxford University Press.
Seamus Heaney *Beowulf, a new translation*, lines 722–8, copyright © Seamus Heaney, 1999.
Reprinted by permission of Faber and Faber.

# Contents

Time Travellers 4

Language Families 6

Before English 8

Invaders 9

Old English 10

Next – the Vikings 14

All change 16

Then the Normans 18

Long live Latin! 20

… and Greek! 21

Words from the New World 22

Words from the East 23

Making New Words 24

Words which Tell a Story 26

Words without a Story 27

Mini-dictionary of Word Origins 28

This shows the dates at which the time machine has stopped.

This shows you where to find the mini-dictionary.

## The Time Travellers

**Shaz** is short for *Sharon* and is from Hebrew, the language of the Jewish people. *Sharon* was originally the name of a fertile plain in Israel in Old Testament times.

**Brian** is a Celtic name, coming either from *brigh* meaning 'high' or 'noble', or *bri* meaning 'strong'.

**Dennis** comes from the name of the Greek god *Dionysus*. Saint Denis lived in the Third Century and became the patron saint of France. But Brian and Shaz named their dog after the cartoon character *Dennis the Menace* – because he is one.

# Time Travellers

Have you ever wondered why some things have the names they do?
For example, why is this called a *sausage*?

What is more, have you ever wondered why *sausage* is spelt the way it is,
and not the way it sounds – *sossij*?

To find the answers to these questions we have
to travel – not only to different countries –
but back in time as well. That's because
words – like *sausage* and many more –
came into English from other,
older languages.

**First stop: France, in the Middle Ages**

4

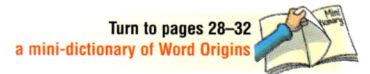

# History in a word

The word *sausage* comes from an Old French word *saussiche.* When the Normans conquered the English in 1066, they brought the word with them. (They may have brought the sausages, too.)

But that's not the start of the story. Sausages go back a long way, and so must we. The Babylonians, the Greeks, and the Romans all ate sausages, and used salt to make them because it preserved the meat.

The Roman language was Latin. The Latin word for *salt* was *sal,* and *salsus* meant 'salted'. From this came *salsicia* meaning 'made with salt': a Latin word for sausages.

France, then called Gaul, was conquered by the Romans and remained part of the Roman Empire for hundreds of years. Because of this, a great many French words came from Latin. Some later found their way into English: *sausage* was just one of them.

The word *sauce* begins with the same three letters as *sausage.* But is that the only connection between them? Find out from the mini-dictionary.

# Language Families

Languages live. They are born, they change, they die. But before they die, new languages grow from them.

Modern English grew from Old English, which grew from an even older language that we call West Germanic. (You can find out why on page 7.)

French grew from Latin, because that was the language of the Roman Empire.

As we travel further back into prehistoric times, we can only guess at the languages people spoke. Historians believe that English belongs to a huge family of languages that all grew – amazingly – from one language spoken about 5,000 years ago.

They call the family **Indo-European**, because so many European and Asian languages belong to it:

Welsh   English   French   Russian
Greek   Hindi   Urdu

You wouldn't think that these languages were all related, but they are. It also means that some of our words may have origins 5,000 years old!

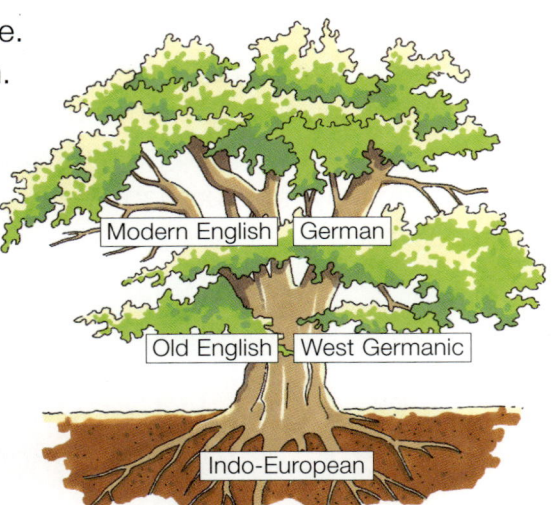

All these words are from different Indo-European languages – living and dead. They all mean the same thing. Find the English word to discover the meaning.

*mayr   macer   mathair   motina*
*matar   meter   mater   madre*
*mere   mother   mutter*

Because they are so alike, they probably all have the same origin.

**Turn to pages 28–32**
a mini-dictionary of Word Origins
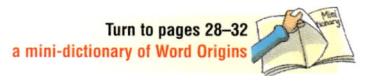

# Family trees

Some Indo-European languages are more closely related than others. There are smaller families inside the big family. This makes some languages 'brothers and sisters' and makes others 'cousins'.

English, German, and Dutch are part of one family. They all have their origins in **West Germanic**.

French, Spanish, Italian, and Portuguese are also closely related. They have their origins in **Latin**.

Many Indian (Indic) languages have their origins in the ancient language of **Sanskrit**.

What is the family connection between Welsh and Irish?
What is the connection between English and Italian?

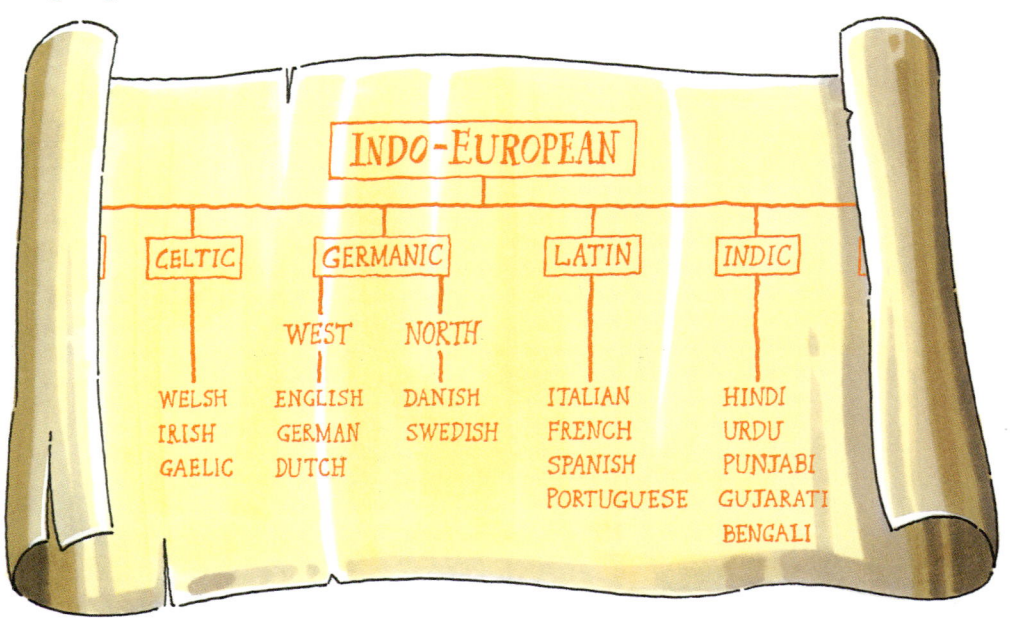

# Mix-up

Old English was a Germanic language. But modern English is a mixture of other languages as well – as you will discover all through this book.

Languages mix when peoples visit each other's lands, either for peaceful reasons, or to invade and conquer. The Romans, the Angles and Saxons, the Vikings, and the Normans all brought words with them that have become part of English.

English-speaking people have also visited or invaded many lands, and brought words back with them, which have added to the English language.

# Before English

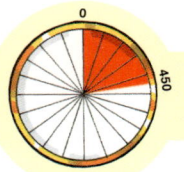

English is not the only language of the British Isles. And it was not the first one.

When the Romans invaded 2,000 years ago, the people they met were called Britons. They spoke a **Celtic** language like Welsh or the Gaelic spoken in Scotland and Ireland.

Only a few English words have Celtic origins. They are the first words for our time travellers, Brian and Shaz, to put in their collection: 

*bin   crag*
*gull   hog*

Have you heard the word *bard*? It is an old word for a poet: William Shakespeare is often called *The Bard*. But the word is much older than that. The Celts, who loved music and story-telling, called their singing poets *bards* – and the title is still given in Wales to winners of poetry festivals.

Some English place names date back to Celtic times. *Carlisle*, *Avon*, and *Pendle* are all Celtic words.

# Invaders

**Turn to pages 28–32**
a mini-dictionary of Word Origins

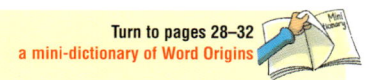

The Romans conquered most of Britain in the First Century AD. They stayed for about three hundred years, and built roads, towns, baths, villas – and much more.
But they didn't leave behind many words.

The Romans did leave some place names. The city of *Lancaster* was a Roman army camp. The Latin for camp was *castra*. So the name Lancaster means 'camp on the River Lune'. The *-chester* in *Manchester* and *Colchester* has the same origin. So does the *-cester* in *Cirencester*.

After the Romans left, Britain was attacked by tribes of Angles, Saxons, and Jutes. For a time the Britons fought back, but in the end they were driven into the north (Scotland) and the west (Devon, Cornwall, Wales, and Ireland).

With them went the Celtic language, and any Latin words which the Britons had learned. In its place came a new, Germanic language – **Anglo-Saxon** – which was to mark the birth of English.

The Angles, Saxons, and Jutes had also lived on the borders of the Roman Empire, and they had picked up some Latin words. These later found their way into English. The Anglo-Saxon words for these things all came from Latin:

*street, sack, pillow, wine, inch, pound, mile…*

*mile*, for example, meant '1000 paces', and came from Latin *milia*, meaning 'thousands'.

Which of the words above came from *strata*, which was Latin for 'spread' or 'laid down'? Check your answer in the mini-dictionary.

# Old English

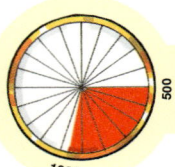

The Angles, Saxons, and Jutes became the new people of England. It was the Angles that gave it its name. The origin of *England* is *Engla-land*, 'the land of the Angles'. And their language was now called *Englisc*.

Engla-land,
Engla-land,
Engla-land

Englisc was a very different language from modern English, so we describe it as **Old English** or **Anglo-Saxon**.

Who invited him?

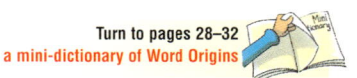
# Beowulf

You can see how different Old English was from this piece of a long poem called *Beowulf*, which was written more than 1,000 years ago.

…Duru sona onarn,
fyrbendum fæst, syþðan he hire folmum æthran;
onbræd þa bealohydig, ða he gebolgen wæs,
recedes muþan. Raþe æfter þon
on fagne flor feond treddode,
eode yrremod; him of eagum stod
ligge gelicost leoht unfæger.

The writer is describing how the monster, Grendel, breaks into a great hall where the warriors are sleeping. Here is Seamus Heaney's modern translation.

Can you find the Old English words for *door*, *floor*, *eyes*, and *light* in these lines from *Beowulf*? Use the mini-dictionary to help you.

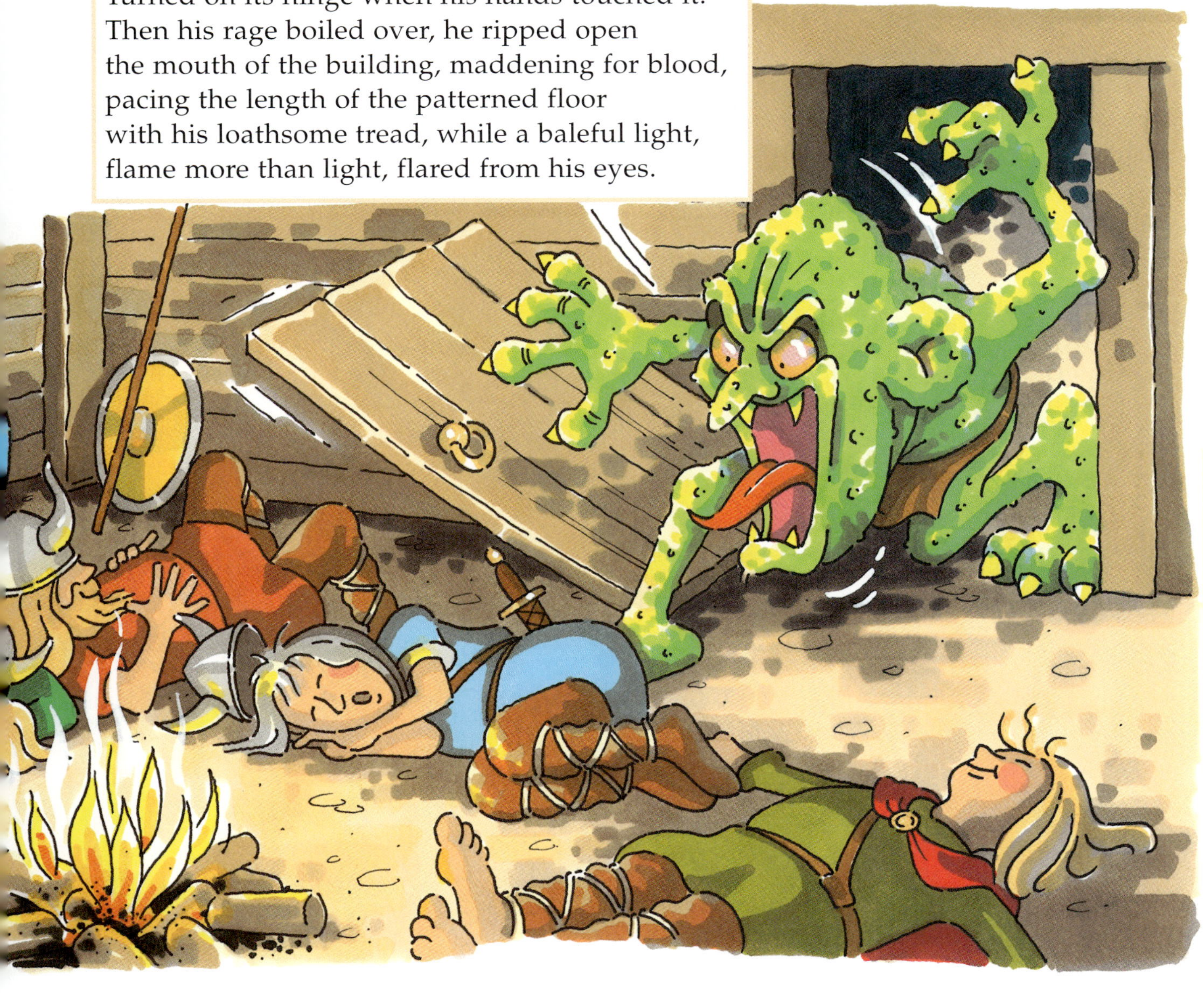

…The iron braced door
Turned on its hinge when his hands touched it.
Then his rage boiled over, he ripped open
the mouth of the building, maddening for blood,
pacing the length of the patterned floor
with his loathsome tread, while a baleful light,
flame more than light, flared from his eyes.

# The roots of everyday words

Many of our most ordinary, everyday words go back to Old English. Here are some that Shaz and Brian collected.

The way the word may have sounded is in brackets.

eat was etan (ay-tan)
sleep was slepan (slay-pan)
house was hus (hoos)
build was byldan (bildan)
head was heafod (hayer-fod)
foot was fot (foat)
ship was scip (ship)
bridge was brycg (bridge)

Brian has learnt that Shaz is his *sweoster*, that he is her *brothor*, and that Dennis is their *hund*. Dennis starts to *beorcan*, just to prove it.

They are given a *mæl* of *fisc* and *bread* with *meolc* to drink, sitting at a long *bord* in the *hus*. They are invited to stay for the *niht*, though they have to *slepan* with a *sceap* and a *cu*.

**Turn to pages 28–32**
**a mini-dictionary of Word Origins**

The man of the house where Brian and Shaz stay is called the *hlaford*, and his wife is called the *hlafdig*. These are the origins of our words *lord* and *lady*, but Shaz is surprised to find what they meant then. Try looking them up in the mini-dictionary.

The word *table* hasn't come into English yet. The Anglo-Saxon word was *bord*. We still use it sometimes, for example *board and lodging*.

Don't you if and but with me!

The spelling of Old English sounds was not the same as ours. For example,
**-sc-** was pronounced like our **-sh-**. Find and say some Old English words on this page with this sound in them.

Most of the small words we use to build sentences come from Old English:

*and  but  if  to  from*
*here  there  over  under*
*this  that*

# Next – the Vikings

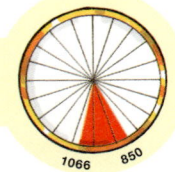

England, and its new language, had little time to settle down before another invasion began. This time it was the Vikings from Norway and Denmark.

The Vikings – or Norsemen or Danes as they were also called – were related to the Anglo-Saxons. They could even understand each other's languages – though it didn't mean they were friends!

At first the Vikings just made savage raids and then went home again. But in 850 they came to England to stay. After nearly thirty years of fighting, they made a deal: the Danes would rule one half of the country and the Anglo-Saxons the other.

Norway

North Sea

Denmark

Britain

The parts of England ruled by the Vikings were called the Danelaw.

Which parts of England did the Danes control? Why do you think this was?

14

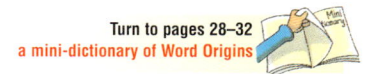

# Old Norse, new words

The language the Viking settlers spoke was **Old Norse**. Here are some examples:

*lift   take   dirt   leg   sky   freckle*

Many Old Norse words found their way into English during this time, as the two peoples mixed. Sometimes a Norse word would take the place of an English one. But sometimes both words remained, so that there were two ways of saying the same thing. For example:

**ditch** from Old English *dic*          **dike** from Old Norse *dik*

Today, even though they are used in slightly different ways, **ditch** and **dike** still mean roughly the same.

**husbondi**

**wif**

Here's an interesting couple: *husband* came from Old Norse *husbondi* and meant 'master of the house' (*hus*); *wife* came from Old English *wif* meaning 'woman'.

15

# All change

The time travellers want to buy something to wear from the Ninth Century – just to prove they've been there. Shaz is looking for a *skirt* and Brian wants a *shirt*. But to their surprise, they find there is no difference.

*shirt* (from Old English *scyrte*)　　*skirt* (from Old Norse *skyrta*)

Shaz and Brian are finding out that words can change their meanings as time goes by. Once *shirt* and *skirt* were two words for the same thing. Now they mean completely different things.

Turn to pages 28–32
a mini-dictionary of Word Origins

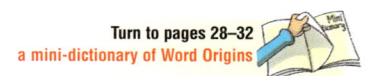

Many more Old Norse words have changed their meanings since they first came into the English language. For example:

*score    stagger    awkward    window*
*anger    scales    scare*

Look up these words in the mini-dictionary. How have they changed?

There is one famous traditional tale that would not be the same without these two Old Norse words:

*uggligr – ugly    troll – troll*

What's the name of the fairy tale? Find out if these words have always had these meanings.

# Then the Normans

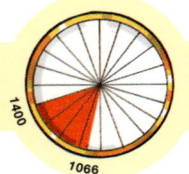

In 1066 William, Duke of Normandy became 'William the Conqueror' by defeating King Harold at the Battle of Hastings. He also became the king of England.

William was a Norman. The Normans (which meant 'north-men') were Vikings who had settled in France two hundred years before. But they no longer spoke the Norse language. The language that William brought to England was **Norman French**.

After the conquest, all the important jobs, and most of the land, went to the Normans. So for a long time the top people in England spoke French, and the ordinary people spoke English. It stayed like that for nearly three hundred years during the Middle Ages. Yet, in the end, the English language was the one that survived.

But English was now a very different language. For a start, thousands of French words had been added to it. Its grammar had changed too. So, it was no longer Old English, but a language that the historians call **Middle English**.

Here is a piece of Middle English, written by the poet Geoffrey Chaucer in about 1400. It tells how a knight called Palamon escapes from prison.

…soon after the mydnyght Palamoun
By helping of a friend, brak his prisoun
And fleeth the citee faste as he may go.

How would you write this part of *The Knight's Tale* if you were using modern English?

**Turn to pages 28–32**
a mini-dictionary of Word Origins
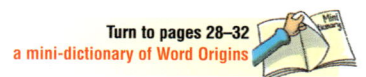

# Power words

Because French was the language of the important people, lots of words to do with law and government came from French:

*justice  jury  parliament  duke  duchess  mayor  royal  court  prison …*

So did many words that richer people would have used:

*mansion  manor  feast  satin  robe  butler  carpet  cushion …*

And a lot of words to do with cooking came from French – as you might expect:

*supper  dinner  roast  boil  soup  sausage  gravy  beef  pork  mutton  custard  cream  sugar*

**Synonyms** are words which mean the same – or nearly the same – as each other.

For example, *sight* and *vision* are synonyms:

*sight* comes from Old English *sihth* and became *sight* in Middle English. (This also explains its peculiar spelling.)

*vision* was Old French, and came from Latin *visio*, meaning 'seeing'.

Modern English is full of synonyms like these. Here are some more.

*depart/leave     help/aid     ancient/old*

Guess which is the Old English word in each pair and which is the Old French. Check their origins in the mini-dictionary.

# Long live Latin!

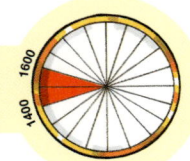

Latin died out as a spoken language in the Middle Ages. But many Latin words lived on in other languages – including English.

As you know, the word *sausage* came from Latin by way of French. So did the words *mountain, lake, flower, bottle, poison, story,* and a great many more.

Brian and Shaz investigated the words *bottle* and *poison*, which they found in a fifteenth-century poem, called *The Pardoner's Tale* by Geoffrey Chaucer. It is about three friends who try to cheat and kill each other to gain money. One of them goes…

> …Into the nexte strete unto a man,
> And from hym borwed large botelles thre
> And in the two his poyson poured he

Of course, all three friends meet with a bad end.

Can you spot the words for *bottle* and *poison* in the poem? Find out more about their origins from the mini-dictionary.

Also look up *mountain, lake,* and *flower*. And check the story behind *story*.

Latin lived on in another way too. Many books were written in Latin, and it was also the language of the Christian Church. It was taught in schools and all educated people were expected to learn it. So many Latin words, like these, became part of English:

| | | |
|---|---|---|
| *exit* | *circus* | *fungus* |
| *plus* | *minus* | *junior* |

Did these all have the same meanings in Latin that they have now? Check them in the mini-dictionary.

# ... and Greek!

**Turn to pages 28–32**
a mini-dictionary of Word Origins

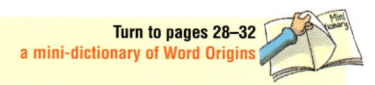

The word *school* comes from the Greek word *skhole*. The Romans made it *schola.* In Old English it was *scol*: another example of why a lot of English words have funny spelling!

Many English words have origins in ancient Greece. For example:

*zone   chaos   idea   orchestra*

are all Greek words, though some of their meanings have changed. The mini-dictionary will show you how.

In ancient Greece an *akrobatos* was someone who walked on tiptoe. From it comes our word *acrobat*. Many more words to do with entertainment come from Greek:

*comedy   theatre   music   drama*

Many of the subjects we learn in school were given names that came from Greek or Latin:

*history   science   geography   mathematics*

Which of the subject names above are from Latin?
Which are from Greek?

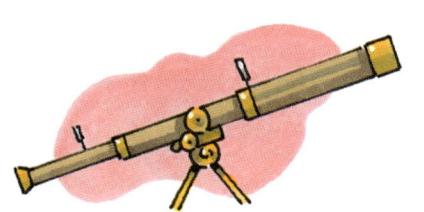

Historians call the end of the Middle Ages the **Renaissance**. It was a time of great activity in art and science, when people again looked back to ancient Greece and Rome for ideas. This is one reason why so many Greek and Latin words were added to English at this time.

# Words from the New World

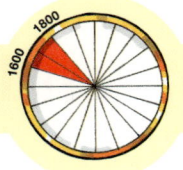

In 1492 Christopher Columbus crossed the Atlantic Ocean with three ships and landed on the islands of the Caribbean. Other explorers and settlers soon followed, from many European countries, including the 'Pilgrim Fathers' from England who settled in what is now the United States of America.

The European explorers took their own languages with them, but they also borrowed words from the different languages of the Amerindians, the original people of America. Several **Amerindian** words have become part of English, especially words for things the explorers had never seen before – like *potatoes* or *llamas*.

*tomato   chilli   cashew   chocolate   tobacco   jaguar puma   skunk   caribou (reindeer)   hammock   barbecue moccasin   toboggan*

Not all these words came straight into English. For example, *tomato* came from Spanish; but originally it was from a Mexican word, *tomatl*.

Find out more about the other words in the list in the mini-dictionary.

## Exploring for words

Later explorations of the South Seas gave English yet more new words.

From Australia: *boomerang budgerigar   kangaroo   koala*

From New Zealand: *kiwi*

From the island of Tahiti: *tattoo*

And from Hawai: *ukulele*

A *ukulele* is a very small guitar that came from Portugal. The Hawaiians nick-named it 'jumping flea', which was *ukulele* in their own language. And the name stuck.

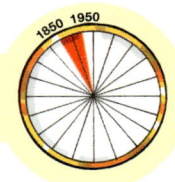

# Words from the East

Turn to pages 28–32
a mini-dictionary of Word Origins

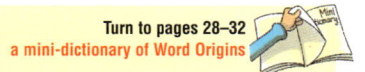

For over a hundred years the British were the rulers of India. During that time many British people went to live in India, and often used words from the languages they heard there. Many of these have come to be part of English.

The following words came from the Indian languages of **Hindi** and/or **Urdu**:

*cot shampoo loot jungle dinghy chutney khaki pyjamas shawl dungarees*

The English had no word for a low, single-storey house until they borrowed *bangla* from an Indian language, and spelt it the way it sounded: *bungalow*.

Find out from the Brian and Shaz's mini-dictionary what *khaki* and *pyjamas* meant in their original language.

## And from the Far East

Similarly, as British people travelled and settled further east, new words from Chinese and Japanese languages were borrowed into English.

These words came from Chinese languages:
*tea typhoon wok ketchup*

These words came from Japanese:
*judo karate soya karaoke tycoon*

Check the origins of these words in the mini-dictionary.

# Making New Words

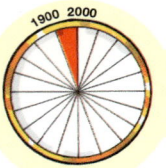

No living language stays the same forever. All the time new words are being added, and old ones are changing or disappearing. But where do new words come from? Who makes them up, and why?

One reason for new words is that new things are invented or discovered and so new words are needed to describe them, for example *airport*. A hundred years ago no planes were flying. There were *ports* for ships, but no such thing as an *airport*. The word did not exist.

Hundreds of new inventions during the last century needed new words to name them. Here are just a few:

| | | |
|---|---|---|
| *helicopter* | *television* | *video* |
| *fax* | *microwave* | *laser* |
| *burger* | *minibus* | *Internet* |

Find out from the mini-dictionary how the words *laser* and *Internet* were made.

**television**

**video**

**lorry**

**burger**

24

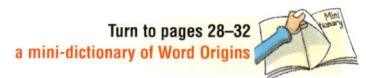

# Compound words

However, very few words are completely new. Usually they are put together from other, older words.

As we have seen, *airport* was made by joining, *air + port*. Both these words are very old, but *airport* wasn't heard until 1919.

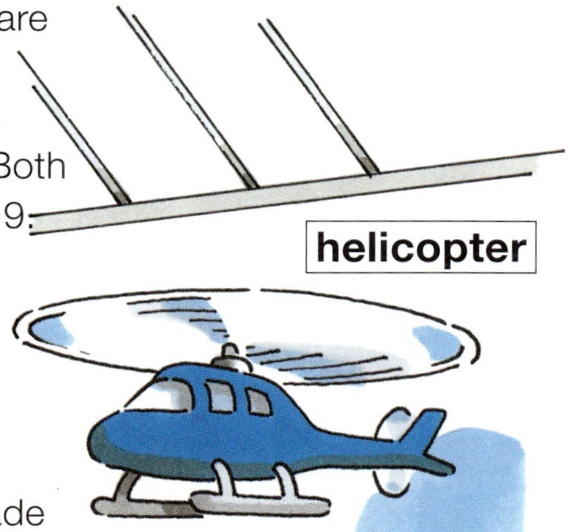

Look up *airport* in the mini-dictionary and find out how far back these words go.

Words like *airport*, which are made from shorter words, are called **compound words**. Many new English words are made in this way, for example:

*hovercraft*     *spaceship*     *funfair*     *fireworks*     *windscreen*

Discover from the mini-dictionary how two of these compound words were put together.

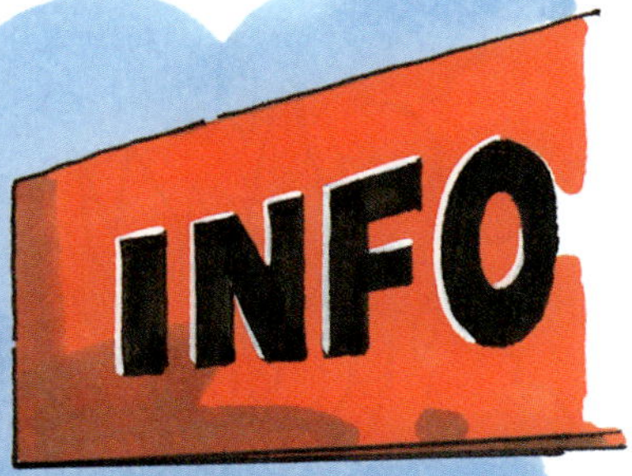

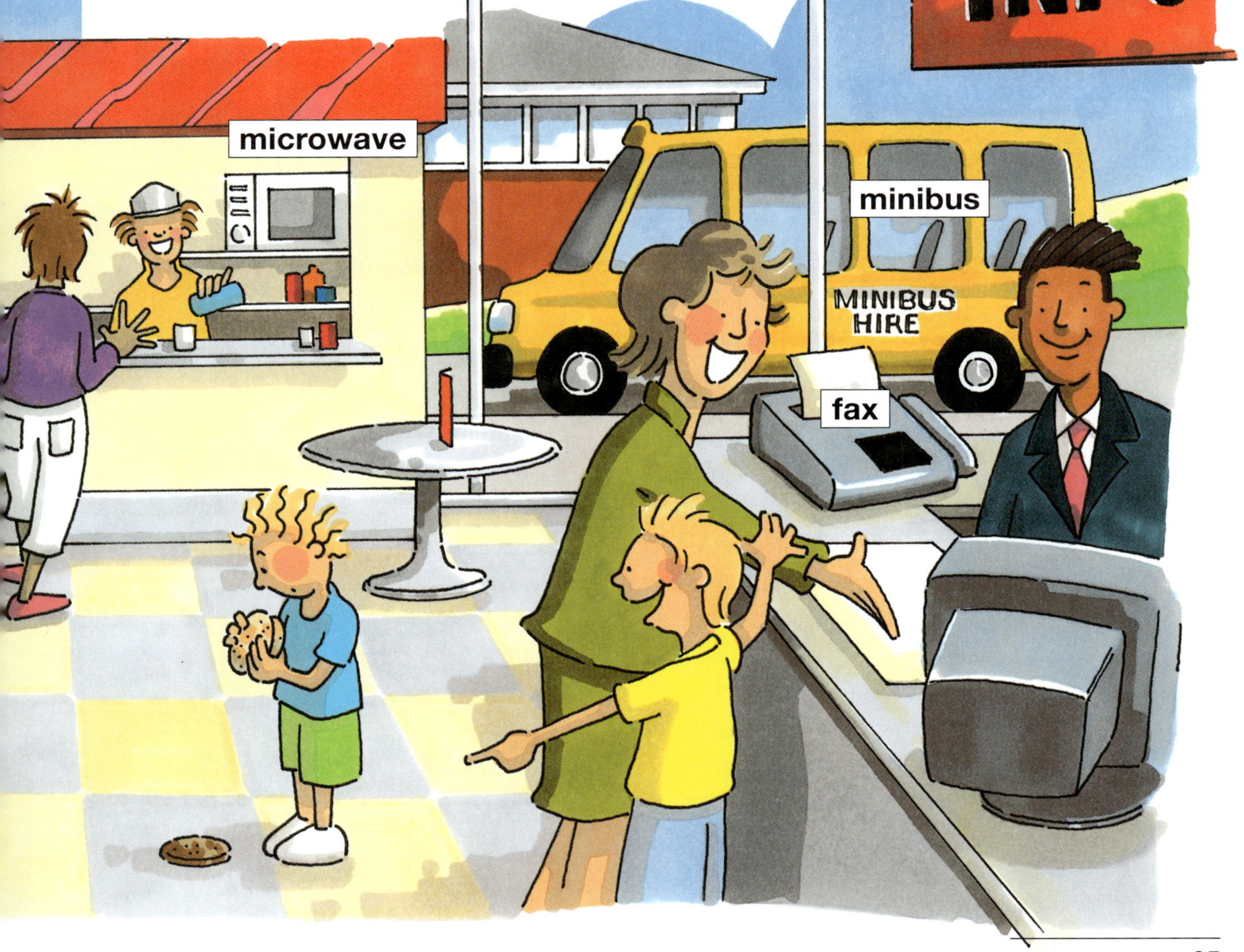

helicopter

INFO

microwave

minibus

MINIBUS HIRE

fax

# Words which Tell a Story

Next time you hear a *siren* – blaring from a police car or fire engine – think of the Greek legend of the *Seiren*. These were women whose beautiful singing voices caused shipwrecks by luring sailors on to rocks. So *siren* has come to mean 'a wailing sound that warns of danger'. Many other words tell a story like this.

A *bonfire* is now used to mean any outdoor fire, but in Middle English it was a *banefyre* – a special fire in which bones were burned. Nice!

*Wellies* is short for *Wellington boots*, named after the Duke of Wellington who wore knee-high boots.

People who compete against each other are *rivals*. The word comes from *rivalis*, the Latin for 'a person who gets water from the same river as someone else'.

The words *apron* and *adder* (the snake), have the same curious story behind them. They were once *naperon* and *nadder*. But when people said *a naperon* it sounded just like *an apron*. Try saying *a nadder* as well.

John Montagu, who was the Earl of Sandwich in the Eighteenth Century, used to eat meat in between two slices of bread. Many people at the time thought this a strange eating habit, but can you guess which word came from it? Check your answer in the mini-dictionary.

# Words without a Story

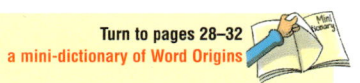Turn to pages 28–32
a mini-dictionary of Word Origins

Some words seem to come from nowhere: their origins are unknown. For example:

*badge*      *blizzard*      *donkey*      *jump*

Another word with unknown origins is *gadget*, which, of course, means any clever tool or piece of equipment. It was a word that sailors started using in the Nineteenth Century, but no one knows where it first came from. As ships travel all over the world, it could have been picked up anywhere!

# Mini-dictionary of Word Origins

## Word origins and dictionaries

We have come to the end of Brian and Shaz's journey through time. The words they collected on their travels have been made into the mini-dictionary below.

It is a dictionary of word origins which explains what is known about the history of the words. You can find information about word origins in many other dictionaries, too.

Knowing the history of a word can often help you to understand it better. It can also help a lot with spelling, since many of the weird spellings of English words are explained when you know their origins.

## Brian and Shaz's time-travellers' mini-dictionary

**acrobat** from Greek *akrobatos* meaning 'walking on tiptoe'.

**adder** from Old English; originally called *a nadder*, which became *an adder*.

**aid** from Old French *aidier*.

**airport** compound word: **air** (from Old French) + **port** (from Latin *portus* meaning 'harbour').

**ancient** from Old French.

**anger** from Old Norse *angr*, meaning 'grief'.

**apron** originally *a naperon*, from French *nappe* meaning 'tablecloth'.

**awkward** from an Old Norse word *afugr*, meaning 'turned the wrong way', with -ward added to it.

**badge** origin unknown.

**barbecue** from a word in a Caribbean language meaning 'wooden frame on posts'.

**bard** from a Celtic word, known to have been used 2000 years ago.

**bark** from Old English *beorcan*.

**beak** from Old French, of Celtic origin.

**beef** from Old French *boef*.

**bin** via Old English from a Celtic word.

**blizzard** origin unknown.

**boil** from an Old French verb.

**bonfire** from a Middle English word *banefyre* = **bone** + **fire**.

**boomerang** an Australian Aboriginal word.

**bottle** from Middle English *botel*, from Old French *botaille*, from Latin *buttis* meaning 'cask'.

**bridge**  from Old English *brycg*.

**brother**  from Old English *brothor*.

**budgerigar**  an Australian Aboriginal word.

**build**  from Old English *byldan*.

**bungalow**  from Hindi *bangla* meaning 'coming from Bengal'.

**burger**  short for *hamburger* which meant 'from Hamburg', a city in Germany. (It had nothing to do with ham: the meat was beef!)

**butler**  from Old French *bouteillier* meaning 'cup bearer'.

**caribou**  from a Native American word meaning 'snow-shoveller' (because the caribou scrapes away the snow to feed on the grass underneath).

**carpet**  from Old French.

**cashew**  via Portuguese from Tupi (a South American language).

**chaos**  from Greek, meaning 'huge pit' or 'chasm'.

**chilli**  via Spanish from Nahuatl (a Central American language).

**chocolate**  via French or Spanish from Nahuatl (a Central American language).

**chutney**  from Hindi *chatni*.

**circus**  from Latin, meaning 'ring'.

**comedy**  from Greek *komos* meaning 'celebration' + *aoidos* meaning 'singer'.

**cot**  from Hindi *khat* meaning 'bedstead'.

**court**  from Old French.

**cow**  from Old English *cu*.

**crag**  a Celtic word.

**cream**  from Old French.

**cushion**  from Old French.

**custard**  from Old French.

**dazzle**  from Old Norse *dasathr* meaning 'weary', same origin as *dazed*.

**depart**  from Old French *départir* meaning 'separate'.

**dike**  from Old Norse *dik*.

**dinghy**  from Hindi *dingi*.

**dinner**  from Old French *disner* which meant 'dine'.

**dirt**  from Old Norse.

**ditch**  from Old English *dic*.

**dog**  from Old English *docga*.

**donkey**  origin unknown.

**door**  from Old English *duru*.

**drama**  from Greek.

**duchess**  from Old French *duchesse*.

**duke**  from Old French *duc*, from Latin *dux* meaning 'leader'.

**dungarees**  from Hindi *dungri* meaning the cloth they were made of.

**eat**  from Old English *etan*.

**exit**  Latin, meaning 'he or she goes out'.

**eye**  from Old English *eage* (*eagum* was a plural form).

**fax**  short for **facsimile**, from Latin *fac* meaning 'make' + *simile* meaning 'a likeness'.

**feast**  from Old French *feste* meaning 'feast'.

**fireworks**  a compound word: **fire** + **work**.

**fish**  from Old English *fisc*.

**floor**  from Old English *flor*.

**flower**  from Old French, from Latin *flos* meaning 'flower'. (The plural was *flores*.)

**foot**  from Old English *fot*.

**freckle**  from Old Norse.

**funfair**  a compound word: **fun** (origin unknown) + **fair** (from Latin *feria* meaning 'holiday').

**fungus**  Latin.

**gadget**  originally a sailors' word; origin not known for sure.

**geography**  from Greek *geo-* meaning 'earth' and *graphein* meaning 'write'.

**gravy**  from Old French.

**gull**  a Celtic word.

**hammock**  via Spanish from Taino (a South American language).

**head**  from Old English *heafod*.

**helicopter**  from Greek *helix* meaning 'coil' and Greek *pteron* meaning 'wing'.

**help**  from Old English *helpan*.

**history**  from Latin *historia* which came from Greek *historia*, meaning 'learning' or 'finding out'.

**hog**  probably from a Celtic language.

**hound**  from Old English *hund* (*hound* was replaced by *dog* in later centuries).

**house**  from Old English *hus*.

**hovercraft**  a compound word from **hover** (origin unknown) + **craft** (from Old English).

**husband**  from Old Norse *husbondi* meaning 'master of the house'.

**idea**  from Greek.

**inch**  Old English *ynce*, from Latin *uncia* meaning 'a twelfth'.

**Internet**  from prefix **inter** (from Latin meaning 'between') + **net**.

**jaguar**  via Portuguese from a South American language.

**judo**  from Japanese *ju* meaning 'gentle' + *do* meaning 'way'.

**jump**  dates from the Sixteenth Century, but its origin is unknown.

**jungle**  from Hindi *jangal*. (In the old Indian language of Sanskrit, *jangala* meant 'desert' or 'forest'.)

**junior**  Latin meaning 'younger'.

**jury**  from Latin *jurare* meaning 'take an oath'.

**justice**  from Latin *justus*.

**kangaroo**  an Australian Aboriginal word.

**karaoke**  Japanese.

**karate**  from Japanese *kara* meaning 'empty' + *te* meaning 'hand'.

**ketchup**  probably from Chinese *k'e chap* meaning 'tomato juice'.

**khaki**  from Urdu *khaki* meaning 'dust-coloured'.

**kiwi**  a Maori word from New Zealand.

**koala**  an Australian Aboriginal word.

**lady**  from Old English *hlaefdige* from 'person who makes the bread' (compare **lord**).

**lake**  from Old French *lac*, from Latin *lacus*.

**laser**  from the initials of 'Light Amplification (by) Stimulated Emission (of) Radiation'.

**leave**  from Old English *laefan*.

**leg**  from Old Norse *leggr*.

**lift**  from Old Norse *lypta*.

**light**  from Old English *leoht*.

**llama**  via Spanish from Quechua (a South American language).

**loaf**  from Old English *hlaf*.

**loot**  from Hindi.

**lord**  from Old English *hlaford* which meant 'person who keeps the bread' (see **loaf** and compare **lady**).

**major**  Latin meaning 'greater' or 'larger'.

**manor** from Old French; related to **mansion**.

**mansion** from Latin *mansio* meaning 'a place to stay'.

**mathematics** from Greek *mathematike*.

**mayor** from Old French *maire*; related to **major**.

**meal** from Old English *mael*, meaning 'occasion for eating'.

**microwave** from Greek *mikros* meaning 'small' + **wave**.

**mile** from Latin *milia* which meant thousands (of paces).

**milk** from Old English *meolc*.

**minibus** from **mini-** short for **miniature** (from Italian) + **bus**, short for *omnibus*, from Latin meaning 'for everybody'.

**minus** Latin meaning 'less'.

**moccasin** a Native American word.

**mother** from Old English *modor*.

**mountain** from Old French *montaigne*, from Latin *mons* (plural *montes*).

**music** from Greek *mousike* meaning 'of the Muses', who were goddesses of the arts and sciences.

**mutton** via Old French, from a Celtic word.

**night** from Old English *niht*.

**old** from Old English *ald*.

**orchestra** from a Greek word for the space where the chorus danced during a play.

**over** from Old English.

**parliament** from French *parler* meaning 'speak'.

**pillow** via Old English, from Latin.

**plus** from the Latin word meaning *more*.

**poison** from Middle English, from Old French. Its origin is Latin *potio*, meaning 'drink'.

**pork** from Old French *porc*, from Latin *porcus* meaning 'pig'.

**potatoes** via Spanish from Taino (a South American language).

**pound** from Old English *pund*, from Latin *pondo* – a weight of about 12 ounces.

**prison** Old French *prisun*, from Latin *prensio*.

**puma** via Spanish from Quechua (a South American language).

**pyjamas** from Persian or Urdu *pay* which meant 'leg' + *jamah* which meant 'clothing'.

**rival** from Latin *rivalis* which meant someone using the same stream (from *rivus* which meant stream).

**roast** via Old French from Germanic.

**robe** via Old French from Germanic.

**royal** from Old French *roial*, from Latin *regalis*.

**sack** from Old English *sacc*, originally from Latin.

**sandwich** invented by the Earl of Sandwich (1718–92) so that he could eat while he was gambling.

**satin** via Old French from Arabic.

**sauce** from Middle English, and before that from the Latin *salsus* meaning 'salted'.

**sausage** from Old French *saussiche*, from Latin *salsus* meaning 'salted'.

**scales** from Old Norse *skal* meaning 'bowl'.

**scare** from an Old Norse word meaning 'frighten'.

**school**  from Old English *scol*, from Latin *schola*, from Greek *skhole*.

**science**  from Latin *scientia* meaning 'knowledge'.

**score**  from Old Norse meaning a 'notch' or 'cut', used to help in counting.

**shampoo**  originally meaning 'massage' from Hindi *champo* meaning 'press'.

**shawl**  from Persian or Urdu.

**sheep**  from Old English *sceap*.

**ship**  from Old English *scip*.

**shirt**  from Old English *scyrte*.

**sight**  from Old English *sihth*.

**siren**  named after the Seirens in Greek legend, women who by their sweet singing lured seafarers to shipwreck on the rocks.

**sister**  from Old English *sweoster*.

**skirt**  from Old Norse *skyrta*.

**skunk**  a Native American word.

**sky**  from Old Norse.

**sleep**  from Old English *slepan*.

**soup**  from Old French.

**soya**  via Dutch from Japanese.

**spaceship**  a compound word: **space + ship**.

**stagger**  from an Old Norse word meaning 'push'.

**story**  see **history**.

**street**  Old English from Latin *strata via* meaning 'paved way', from *stratus* meaning 'laid down'.

**sugar**  via Old French from Arabic *sukkar*.

**supper**  from Old French *soper*.

**take**  from Old Norse.

**tattoo**  from a Polynesian language.

**tea**  via Dutch from Chinese.

**television**  from Greek *tele* meaning 'far' + **vision**.

**theatre**  from Greek *theatron* which meant 'place for seeing things'.

**tobacco**  via Spanish from a Central American language.

**toboggan**  via Canadian French from a Native American language.

**tomato**  via Spanish or Portuguese from Nahuatl (a Central American language).

**troll**  from Old Norse.

**truant**  from Old French, meaning 'criminal', probably of Celtic origin.

**tycoon**  from Japanese *taikun* meaning 'great prince'.

**typhoon**  from Chinese *tai fung* meaning 'great wind', and from Arabic *tufan*.

**ugly**  from Old Norse *uggligr* meaning 'frightening'.

**ukulele**  from Hawaiian, meaning literally 'jumping flea'.

**video**  Latin meaning 'I see'.

**vine**  from Latin *vinum* meaning 'wine', see **wine**.

**vision**  via Old French from Latin.

**wellies**  short for **wellingtons**, named after the first Duke of Wellington, who wore long leather boots.

**wife**  from Old English *wif* which meant 'woman'.

**window**  Old Norse word meaning 'window', made from *vind* which meant 'wind, and *auga* which meant 'eye'.

**windscreen**  a compound word: **wind + screen**.

**wine**  from Latin *vinum* meaning 'wine'.

**wok**  from Chinese.

**zone**  from Greek.